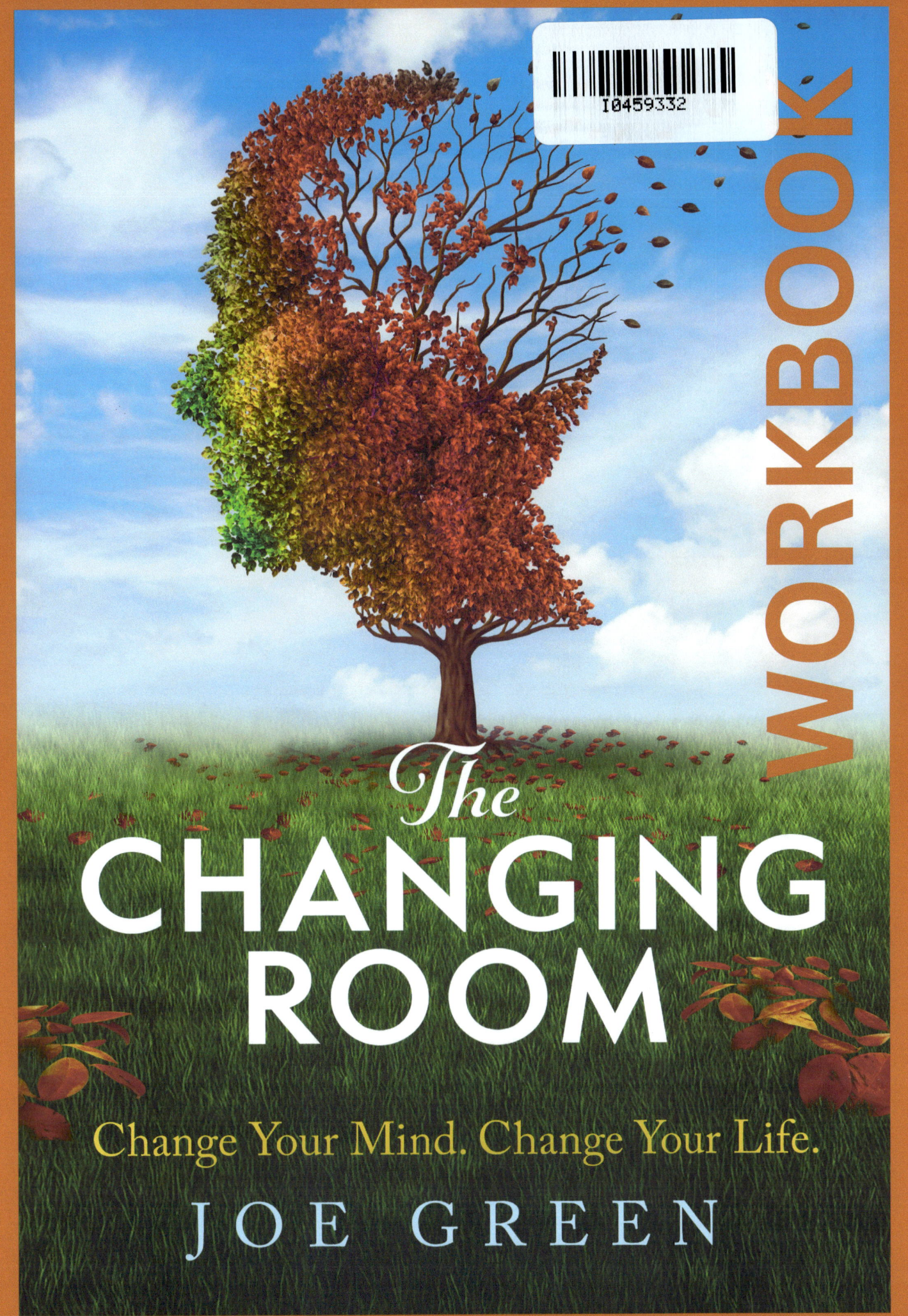

WORKBOOK

The
CHANGING
ROOM

Change Your Mind. Change Your Life.

JOE GREEN

Welcome!

I'm really glad you're here.

This is worth your time.

Sometimes, many times you know when something in your life needs to change. You can feel it. You sense it. You may even talk yourself in and out of it.

But just the thought of change can feel overwhelming.

You're not alone. We've all been there and felt that way at one time or another.

The good news is, it doesn't have to be that way.

There is an art to embracing change, and the process is often very different from what you might expect. This workbook is designed to walk you through the five essential experiences of healthy, sustainable change, one step, one insight, and one decision at a time.

You don't have to have it all figured out. You just have to be willing to begin.

So take a breath, turn the page, and let's step into change together.

Coach Joe

How to Use The Changing Room Workbook

This workbook is your chance to pause, reflect, and explore what's going on in your life right now. There is no right or wrong way to use it — only the way that suits you best.

Feel free to underline, circle words, scratch out notes, or write whatever comes to mind in the moment. The idea is to capture those honest thoughts, inspirations, and real emotions as they arise. This is your chance to check in and get in touch with what you truly want and need going forward.

Take advantage of the sections ahead and use them to help you reflect, reset, and reconnect with yourself.

Change happens one moment at a time. Record those moments on these pages, and over time you will begin to notice patterns, gain clarity, and enjoy the benefits of gaining the kind of insights that really make a difference.

This workbook will quickly become your personal blueprint for self-reflection, motivation, and change.

Take your time, give yourself a chance, and let this workbook meet you exactly where you are every time you use it.

3

PRIVATE SELF REFLECTIONS

PRIVATE SELF-REFLECTIONS

Let's review the purpose of this section and how to get the most out of it.

This section is about self-awareness — taking the time to unpack and explore what's really going on beneath the surface.

Understanding why certain patterns repeat, why some changes feel harder than others, or why certain feelings and emotions continue to show up are all worthwhile pursuits.

Use the pages in this section to "do the math" — to start to figure out how you got to where you are and how to move forward and get unstuck. This is where repeated struggles can begin to reveal powerful opportunities to evolve, to shift perspective, and to attract the kind of positivity you want and need in your life.

Whether you're reflecting on your career, spirituality, relationships, or the challenges you're navigating right now, this is the perfect space to begin to work it out. Capture those random thoughts, the ah-ha moments, and everything in between so that you can get your thoughts out of your head and down on paper.

Don't underestimate the power of written words. When you can see your thoughts clearly, you gain the power to choose differently.

**What is happening in my life for me right now
emotionally, mentally, or situationally?**

(What feels heavy, repetitive, confusing, or unresolved?)

Notes

**What recurring patterns, reactions, or beliefs
do I notice and why is that?**

(Where have I seen this before? What is the lesson(s) to be learned?)

Notes

What clarity, perspective, or next step is beginning to emerge for me?

(Any realization counts.)

Notes

POSITIVE AFFIRMATION REFLECTIONS

POSITIVE AFFIRMATION REFLECTIONS

This section is all about mindset — one of the most powerful influences in our lives.

How you perceive yourself in relationships, in life situations, and through the opinions of others directly impacts your self-esteem, self-confidence, sense of self-worth, and overall well-being.

What you consistently see in your mind's eye often finds its way into your daily routine, sometimes in ways you realize and in other ways that you don't. The truth is, your thoughts — both surface-level and deep within — shape how you show up in the world.

The good news is, you can rewrite that internal script. You can reprogram old beliefs and choose new ones that support you becoming your best self. Changing your mind is one of the greatest freedoms and one of the most powerful privileges we have.

Use this section to practice daily affirmations that strengthen belief in yourself. As your inner dialogue shifts, your confidence grows, your energy changes, and the light around you begins to shine brighter. With intention and consistency, you open yourself to new possibilities in work, relationships, health, and beyond.

Prompts have been included to help guide your reflection and bring awareness to the beliefs and thoughts shaping your mindset.

What thought or belief about myself has been influencing how I show up lately?

(Is it supportive or is it holding me back?)

Notes

**What belief am I ready to release or change and
what would feel more empowering to believe instead?**

(What would I say to myself as if I were giving advice to someone I
really care about?)

Notes

Write an affirmation that feels true, supportive, and aligned with the person you are capable of becoming.

(It doesn't have to be perfect it just has to feel honest.)

Notes

MOTIVATIONAL ACTION QUOTE REFLECTIONS

HOW TO USE THIS SECTION

MOTIVATIONAL ACTION QUOTE REFLECTIONS

Widely regarded as the most popular and powerful section of this workbook, each motivational action quote has something in store for you.

This is a great way to move from contemplating to taking meaningful action right now.

Each quote is like a tap on the shoulder — a reminder to pay attention, refocus, and move what truly matters back to the top of your priority list. This is your chance to reconnect with motivation, confidence, and forward momentum.

Look up the motivational action quotes found at joegreenspeaks.com and use these pages to record your thoughts and inspirations.

Give yourself a few quiet minutes to read the quote and use the pages that follow to capture your thoughts, reactions, and insights. Often, the most powerful breakthroughs begin with a single line that resonates, and the awareness that follows becomes a real gem.

What part of this quote really resonates with me right now?

(What word, phrase, or idea feels personal?)

Notes

**How does this quote inspire me and
what should I pay attention to, rethink, or reprioritize?**

(What might I be overlooking, avoiding, or delaying?)

Notes

**What insight, encouragement or shift in perspective
could I take from this message today?**

(How can this guide my decisions or mindset in the future?)

Notes

TRACTION STEP REFLECTIONS

TRACTION STEP REFLECTIONS

This section is where insight turns into movement.

Awareness creates understanding, but action is what brings change to life. The TrAction steps found on the pages that follow are designed to help you move forward with clarity, purpose, and intention.

Getting started often has less to do with motivation and more to do with knowing what to do next. Clear direction builds confidence, supports sustainability, and helps maintain consistent forward momentum. Regardless of the change you're seeking, having light on the path ahead makes progress feel possible rather than overwhelming.

Use these pages to reflect, commit, and take ownership of your next steps. Real change doesn't require doing everything at once — it begins by choosing one intentional action and taking it.

TRAction Step #1

---◆---

CHANGE ONE THING

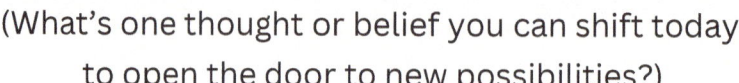

Change Your Mind.
Open your mind to possibilities, believe in yourself and take a chance.

(What's one thought or belief you can shift today
to open the door to new possibilities?)

Notes

_____

_____

_____

_____

_____

_____

_____

_____

_____

_____

_____

_____

_____

_____

_____

_____

Change A Habit.
Change a habit that fails to serve your best interests.
(What habit really needs your attention right now?)

Notes

Change The Norm.
Look for opportunities to respond differently and watch how everyone and everything around gradually changes.
(What thoughts need to change so your life can change for the better?)

Notes

CHANGE REQUIRES VISION

When you are able to see it, change becomes much easier to believe and that belief is what makes change stick.

Take a few minutes each day to quiet your mind, visualize the outcome you want, and let yourself feel it as though it were real. Then, capture your insights, ideas, and inspirations on the pages that follow.

16 MINUTE MEDITATION
Day 1

Incorporate 16 minutes of meditation and/or journaling consistently for the next 5 to 7 days. Commit to this quality time yourself.

....

....

....

....

....

....

....

....

....

....

....

....

....

....

16 MINUTE MEDITATION

Day 2

Incorporate 16 minutes of meditation and/or journaling consistently for the next 5 to 7 days. Commit to this quality time yourself.

16 MINUTE MEDITATION
Day 3

Incorporate 16 minutes of meditation and/or journaling consistently for the next 5 to 7 days. Commit to this quality time yourself.

16 MINUTE
MEDITATION
Day 4

Incorporate 16 minutes of meditation and/or journaling consistently for the next 5 to 7 days. Commit to this quality time yourself.

16 MINUTE
MEDITATION
Day 5

Incorporate 16 minutes of meditation and/or journaling consistently for the next 5 to 7 days. Commit to this quality time yourself.

16 MINUTE MEDITATION
Day 6

Incorporate 16 minutes of meditation and/or journaling consistently for the next 5 to 7 days. Commit to this quality time yourself.

16 MINUTE MEDITATION
Day 7

Incorporate 16 minutes of meditation and/or journaling consistently for the next 5 to 7 days. Commit to this quality time yourself.

TRAction Step #2

———◆———

BECOME BETTER

FAST FORWARD

Self-evolution is one of the most richly rewarding endeavors one can pursue. The journey of continuously pursuing personal growth, as well as breaking down limitations and challenges in order to realize your fullest potential, is both the education and accomplishment of a lifetime.

Get started now with these 5 TrAction Steps to help you become a better version of your former self.

REFLECT

Begin by taking an honest, unfiltered look at yourself. Notice the thoughts, habits, and patterns that define you. Then, focus on what makes you uniquely you—your strengths, talents, and special qualities
Take a moment to honor these gifts, because self-confidence grows when you truly see and appreciate the value you bring to the world.

RECOGNIZE

Search for opportunities to take on new challenges and experiences that will help you grow and improve. Notice the moments that push you outside your comfort zone. These are the moments that spark change and reveal your true potential.
Be open to learning, experimenting, and stretching yourself. Every new experience is a chance to discover strengths you didn't know you had and to move closer to the life you want to create.

FAST FORWARD

Get started now with these 5 TrAction Steps to help you become a better version of your former self.

REINVENT

What you think and say shapes the way you see yourself and the way others see you. Reinvent your thoughts and your words by letting go of limiting beliefs and negative self-talk.
Choose thoughts that empower you, speak with intention, and create the vision of yourself you want to become. Every shift in thinking and language brings you closer to the person you're meant to be.

REFOCUS

Every day is a fresh start, a chance to revisit your goals and pick one action that moves you forward, no matter how big or small. Commit to it and own it.
At the end of the day, pause to review what you accomplished, no matter how small it feels. Celebrate your wins, reflect on what you've learned, and use that insight to set your intention for tomorrow. Consistent, focused action builds momentum, and momentum helps change last.

REALIGN

Choose the company you keep wisely. Replace negativity and distractions with people who lift you up—those who "get it" and truly get you. Surround yourself with support, positivity, and energy that inspires you to be your best self.

notes

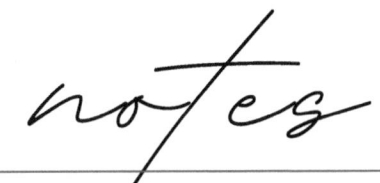

TRAction Step #3

———————◆———————

BELIEVE IN YOURSELF

FOR THE LIFE OF ME

You have the power to choose anything, to try something new, to learn a new way, to discover hidden talents, to take a chance, or to start all over again as many times as you want or need to. Using that power for your own greater good comes down to taking action in a series of steps that I like to refer to as TrAction steps. TrAction steps are a series of well-thought-out, well-intentioned steps that focus your attention and overall awareness on realizing what you really want for yourself. Whether you're deciding on what to do after graduating school, retiring, or during other life transitions, the decision is yours to make.

Try these "Traction Steps" to get started:

IDENTIFY

FOCUS:
Break it down ... who you are, where you're from, where y(ou've been, what you've done and why you need more or something different in your life.

TrAction Step:
Discover the path to what is next by asking yourself where you want to go, what it would take to get there and what you're willing to do to make it happen.

FOR THE LIFE OF ME

Try these "Traction Steps" to get started:

RECOGNIZE

FOCUS:

Understand how and why you have made the choices you've made so far, why you feel the way you do and where it all comes from (childhood, past relationships, or an isolated experience).

TrAction Step:

Finding the answer to your most pressing questions often takes time, patience and a trusted well intentioned unbiased outside opinion to help sort through whatever it is that may be holding you back. Accept the past but leave it where it is because everything and anything you could possibly want is ahead of you.

CLARIFY

FOCUS:

Clearing the path to new beginnings starts with understanding yourself on a deeper level. Being honest and open requires humility. Ego has no place nor any room to reside inside of a mind that is open.

TrAction Step:

Revisit your world, your health, your eating habits, your work ethic, your attitude towards yourself and others and your personal constitution (what you stand for). Take inventory and take the appropriate actions.

FOR THE LIFE OF ME

Try these "Traction Steps" to get started:

INTEND

FOCUS:
Move with intention, start living your life on purpose. Make the first move, start a new chapter, establish a new way of going about the ordinary. Be proactive instead of predictive

TrAction Step:
Without change nothing new can happen. Whether you wait for it or make it happen on your own change is inevitable. Making the decision to create change gives you the chance to customize the experience to your personal liking and desired outcome.

INVENT

FOCUS:
Just by changing your mind you can change your whole entire world. You are exactly (who) you think you are and (what) you think you are.

TrAction Step:
It's never too late to reinvent yourself. Imagine it, create it, see it, be it and then believe it. Who better to write your own story than you? You are the author... You decide how the story goes.
You may have to repeat the steps above several times until you finally get the traction you need but it's well worth it.
Like Mahatma Gandhi said, your life is your message.
... So what's next, what are you going to do with the rest of your life?

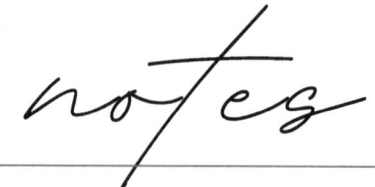

THE POWER OF BEING YOURSELF

Here's a great way to get started on becoming a better version of your former self:

Self-evolution TrAction Steps

STEP 1:
Write down 5 things that describe who you are.

STEP 2: Rate each from 1-10 (1 = Not so good, 5 = Pretty good and 10 = Excellent) along with just a few words to explain why.

STEP 3: Write down the date you wrote this and put it out of sight, somewhere safe.

STEP 4: Revisit this list in exactly 90 days (set a reminder in your phone).

STEP 5: Day 90, retrieve the list and review it.

Jot down today's date and rate yourself again on each of the 5 things that describe you. Be sure to note if there have been any changes, any progress, or setbacks along the way.

Repeat this exercise and add a "can-do" list. This list is comprised of things you can and will do to help improve and continue to progress.

Do this for each of the five things that describe you.
Remember, it's about progress and taking it day by day.
The best part about working within is that it removes the worry and waste of energy wishing and waiting for something great to happen to you.

THE POWER OF BEING YOURSELF

Today's date: _____

**RATE FROM 1-10
(10=BEST)**

**WRITE DOWN 5 THINGS TO
DESCRIBE WHO YOU ARE**

○

○

○

○

○

EXPLAIN YOUR RATINGS

WHY DID YOU RATE YOURSELF THIS WAY?

....

WHY DID YOU RATE YOURSELF THIS WAY?

....

WHY DID YOU RATE YOURSELF THIS WAY?

....

WHY DID YOU RATE YOURSELF THIS WAY?

....

WHY DID YOU RATE YOURSELF THIS WAY?

....

THE POWER OF BEING YOURSELF

90 DAY CHECK-IN

Today's date: _____

**RATE FROM 1-10
(10=BEST)**

**WRITE DOWN 5 THINGS TO
DESCRIBE WHO YOU ARE**

○

○

○

○

○

EXPLAIN YOUR RATINGS

WHY DID YOU RATE YOURSELF THIS WAY?

_____

WHY DID YOU RATE YOURSELF THIS WAY?

_____

WHY DID YOU RATE YOURSELF THIS WAY?

_____

WHY DID YOU RATE YOURSELF THIS WAY?

_____

WHY DID YOU RATE YOURSELF THIS WAY?

_____

TRAction Step #4

---◆---

DISCOVER YOUR STRENGTHS

Self-Identity

You're constantly changing because life is always changing. Your body feels it, and your heart knows it, but sometimes we simply fail to process changes in life and thus lose sight of who we are and what we have become.

Use these TrAction Steps to stay continuously current on who you really are:

STEP 1: Take a moment, look in the mirror, and explain to yourself who you are at home (with family or friends).

STEP 2: Take a moment, look in the mirror, and explain to yourself who you are outside of home (at work, etc).

STEP 3: Take a moment, look in the mirror, and give a detailed description to yourself of your authentic self (include things that very people, few or no one, knows).

Self-reflection is a powerful tool and is the mark of a wisdom seeker. Figuring out who you are, who you want be, or even could be is within your grasp. Start now, find out and be the best possible version of you that you can be.

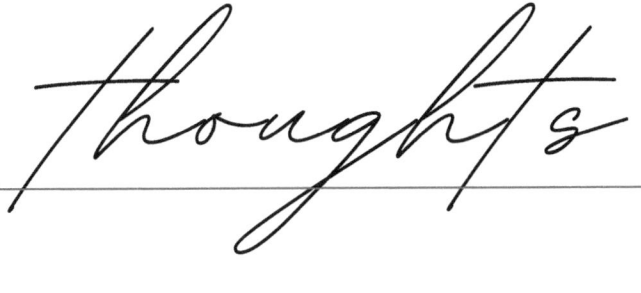

thoughts

TRAction Step #5

———◆———

STAY THE PATH

WHAT'S IN YOUR WAY?

Fear of success is a subconscious, self-imposed obstacle fueled in part by a lack of self-confidence. This kind of fear is limiting, frustrating, controlling, and, more often than not, misunderstood.

Try these TrAction steps to help work through fear of success:

Step
1

TrAction Step

Identify what you believe the obstacles are that are blocking you from successfully reaching your goals.

Step
2

Think about how you feel when it comes to having success, and actually reaching your goals.
Recognize and extinguish limiting beliefs by replacing (fear) an impossibility with a positive possibility... In other words change your thought process.

TrAction Step

REMEMBER YOUR SUCCESS STARTS FROM WITHIN!

Zoe

what's in your way?

what's in your way?

SUIT YOURSELF

Focus and rise above your fears. When you do, it will significantly diminish uncertainty and relieve tension and anxiety.

Try these TrAction steps to sharpen your decision-making powers:

:

Step
1

TrAction Step

Exchange compromise for patience.

Step
2

Replace fear with wisdom.

TrAction Step

Step
3

TrAction Step

Resist negativity with optimism.

SUIT YOURSELF

Focus and rise above your fears. When you do, it will significantly diminish uncertainty and relieve tension and anxiety.

Try these TrAction steps to sharpen your decision-making powers:

:

Step
4

TrAction Step

Denounce doubt; choose determination.

Step
5

Embrace challenge to discover change.

TrAction Step

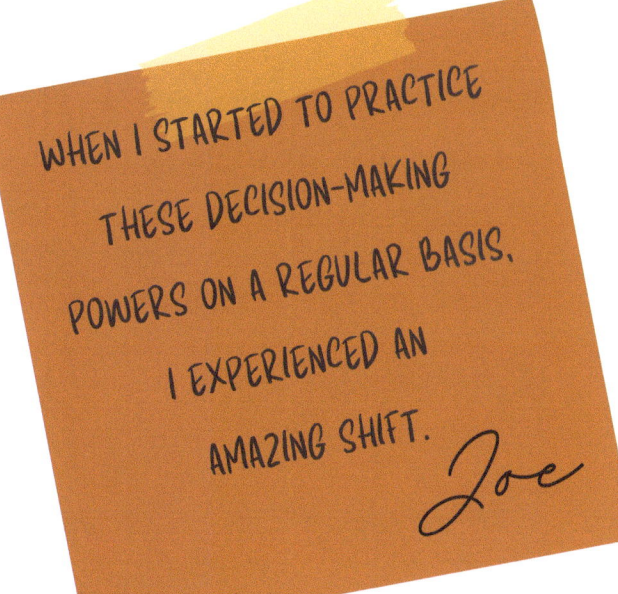

WHEN I STARTED TO PRACTICE THESE DECISION-MAKING POWERS ON A REGULAR BASIS, I EXPERIENCED AN AMAZING SHIFT.

Joe

HERE'S A GREAT WAY TO BRING THE POWER OF YOUR INTENTIONS AND THESE 5 STEPS ALL TOGETHER RIGHT NOW:

Write a letter to your future self.

Give a detailed description of the person you want to be.

Describe the greatest challenges you anticipate facing and how you plan to overcome them.

Then write down the single most limiting belief that you have about yourself and convert it into a positive affirmation.

Next, wrap up with a few sentences describing your strategy for success as well as who and/or what you will be eliminating to help get rid of any unwanted negative energy.

Jot down who or what you will get to replace the negative with positive.

End the letter with this sentence:
"I'm on my way, and I promise, I am worth the wait."
Practice and repeat those action steps daily. Like any worthwhile process, consistency is the secret sauce that brings it all together and makes it work.

You got this!

Dear Me,

CONTINUE THE CONVERSATION

Let it all out here

Let it all out here

Let it all out here

66

Let it all out here

Let it all out here

Let it all out here

Let it all out here

Let it all out here

Let it all out here

Let it all out here

Let it all out here

Let it all out here

Let it all out here

Let it all out here

Let it all out here

This Message is For You!

Each time you use this workbook, take a moment to acknowledge the work you have done. Awareness creates clarity, clarity creates choice, and choice is where change begins.

But it all starts with time, and the time you are investing is time well spent.

The insights and notes you have written reach well beyond these pages. They create a pathway to success, reminding you of what matters and what's possible. Return to this workbook whenever you need grounding, direction, or a space where you can feel free to be your authentic self.

This workbook is your canvas.

It is your companion—a reminder that you don't have to walk this path alone. That is one of the main reasons I created it.

Consider my hand extended as an offer for continued inspiration and support when I say: you are invited to stay connected by signing up to receive my free weekly Motivational Action Quotes. They are short, impactful messages designed to help you stay focused, encouraged, and aligned as you continue creating change.

Scan the QR code or visit:
www.joegreenspeaks.com

Change your mind. Change your life.

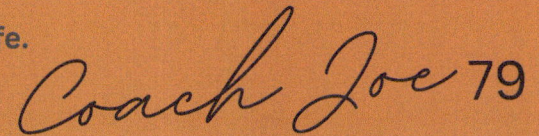

79

Library of Congress Cataloging-in-Publication Data has been applied for this ISBN, 979-8-9998830-0-1

For international rights and translations inquiries, contact: Joe Green
www.joegreenspeaks.com